AMAZING COWS!

AMAZING COWS!

A BOOK OF BOVINELY INSPIRED MISINFORMATION

by

SANDRA BOYNTON

workman

Sandra Boynton's
FUN!
FROLICS!
FASHION!
MAYHEM!

ZING
WS!
STORIES!
JOKES!
POEMS!
COMICS!
UDDER
ABSURDITY!

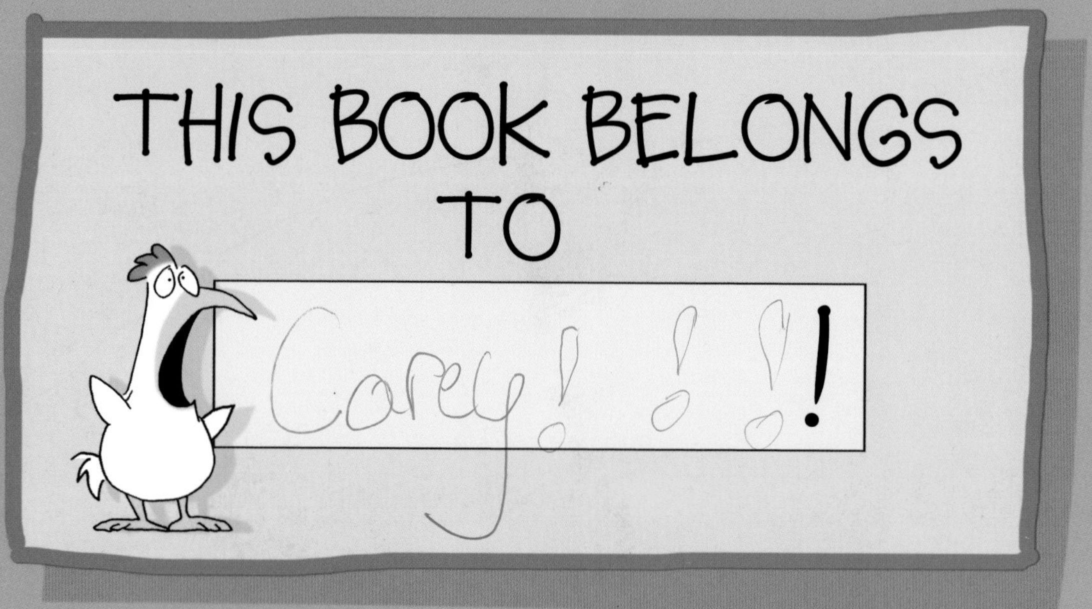

THIS IS FOR YOOOO, AUNT JACKIE!

Published simultaneously in Canada by Thomas Allen & Son Limited.

Library of Congress Cataloging-in-Publication Data is available

ISBN 978-0-7611-6214-8 (pb)
ISBN 978-0-7611-6371-8 (hc)

WORKMAN PUBLISHING COMPANY, INC.
225 Varick St., New York, NY 10014-4381
www.workman.com www.sandraboynton.com
Manufactured in Mexico First Printing October 2010 10 9 8 7 6 5 4 3 2 1

CONTENTS

The Enviable Serenity of Cows

Canooo

INTRODUCTION

THE THING ABOUT COWS

Much has been written about why cows are so widely admired. Or maybe nothing at all has been written about that. We forgot to check.

Figuring out the best explanation for the wild popularity of cows is really a pretty difficult task. Is it their quiet beauty? Is it their simple style? The way they're never moody? The magic of their smile?

It's all these things. In fact, what makes cows most amazing is that they don't have to actually DO anything to be amazing.

They just ARE.

Truly Outstanding in the Field

Of course, the problem with this is that, since they mostly just stand around being amazing and all, there's not really much of anything to put in an entire book about cows.

But that didn't worry us. We just went ahead and made stuff up.

HOW TO SPEAK COW

Most cows, of course, speak English. But when you are visiting cows at home, it is thoughtful and polite to address them in their own language. Here are some useful phrases to know.

Hello!
Moo.

How are you?
Moo.

My name is Floyd.
Moo Floyd.

I like your beanie copter.
Moo.

Do you think it will snow?
Moo?

It was nice talking with you.
Moo.

Good-bye.
Moo revoir.

3 COW JOKES!

Q: Where does a cow get its ideas?

A: From its muuuuse.

Q: How do cows pay for things?

A: With moolah.

Q: What kind of cows have horns?

A: Big Band cows.

COW STORY

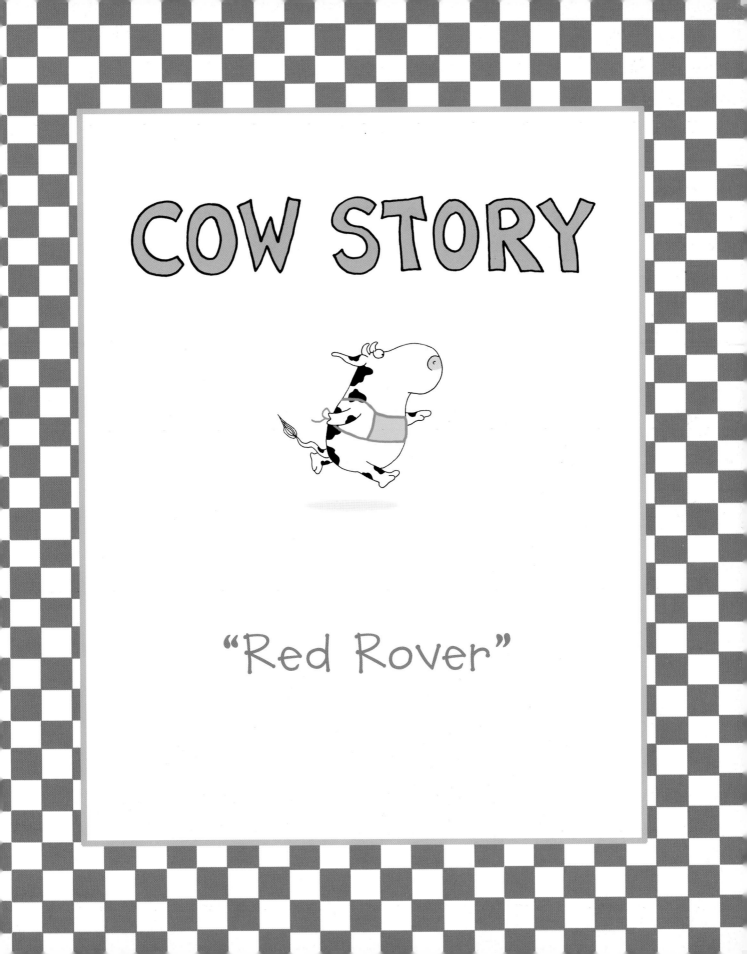

"Red Rover"

COW STORY

Once upon a time, there were 137 cows who lived very happily on a lovely farm in North Dakota or something. Their names were Ezekiel, Ted, Rose, Carumba, Andrew, Mitch, Cucumber, Sly, Simone, Clark, Milo, Gorgonzola, Bipsy, Debit, Louise, Jean-Pierre, Walter,

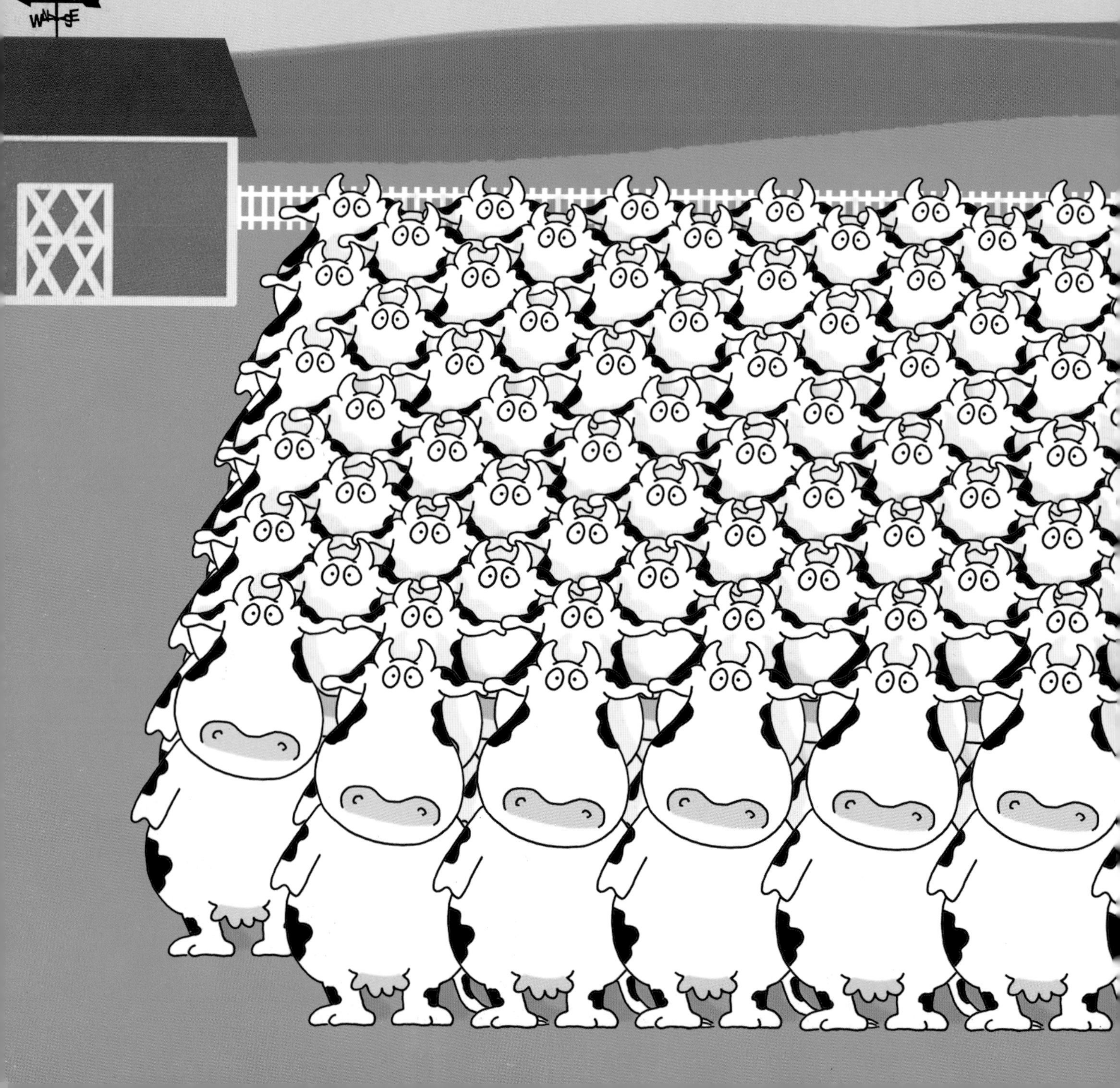

Helicopter, Zorro, Big George, Vladimir, Dave, G. K. Chesterton, Mimi, Lightning, Victor, Larry, Cruise Control, Nell, Azalea, Cookie, Angel, Xavier, Sneaker, Orwell, Trouble, Stanley, Fred, Sofa, Lillian, Ezra, Scooter, Myron, Zippy, Chaos, Daffodil, Buzz, Brewster, Gabby, Dink, Mosquito, Emmy, Trixie, Jupiter, Jeremiah, Tyler, and Steve. The remaining eighty cows were all named Tino, which was not a good idea.

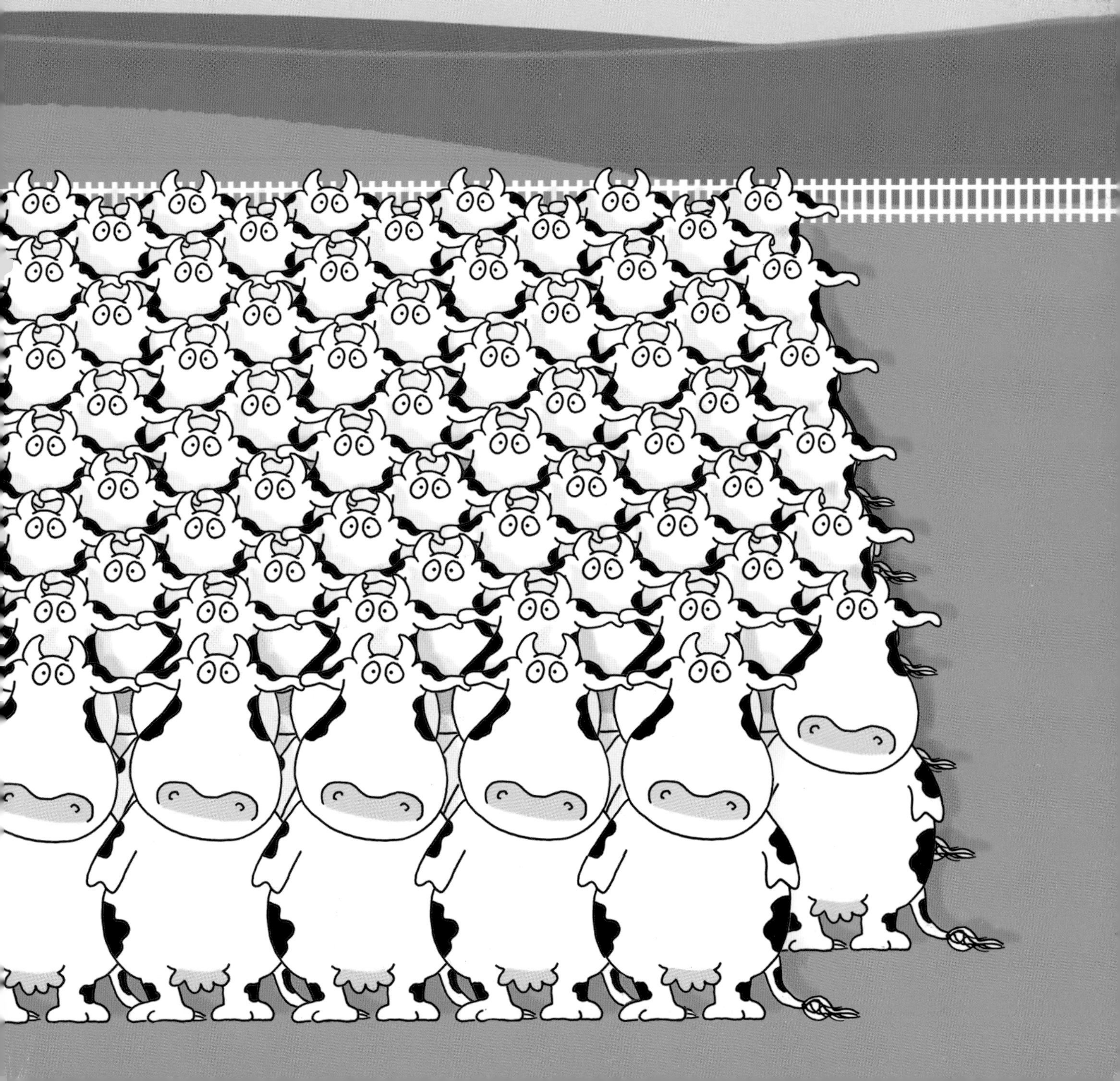

One fine Spring day, three wandering chickens (Chuck, Stuart, and Nedly) happened by the farm and, after telling a few funny cow jokes (see pages 10, 24, and 71), they suggested to the cows (Ezekiel, Ted, Rose, Carumba, Andrew, and so forth) that they all play a friendly game of Red Rover.

The cows were quite smitten with this plan.

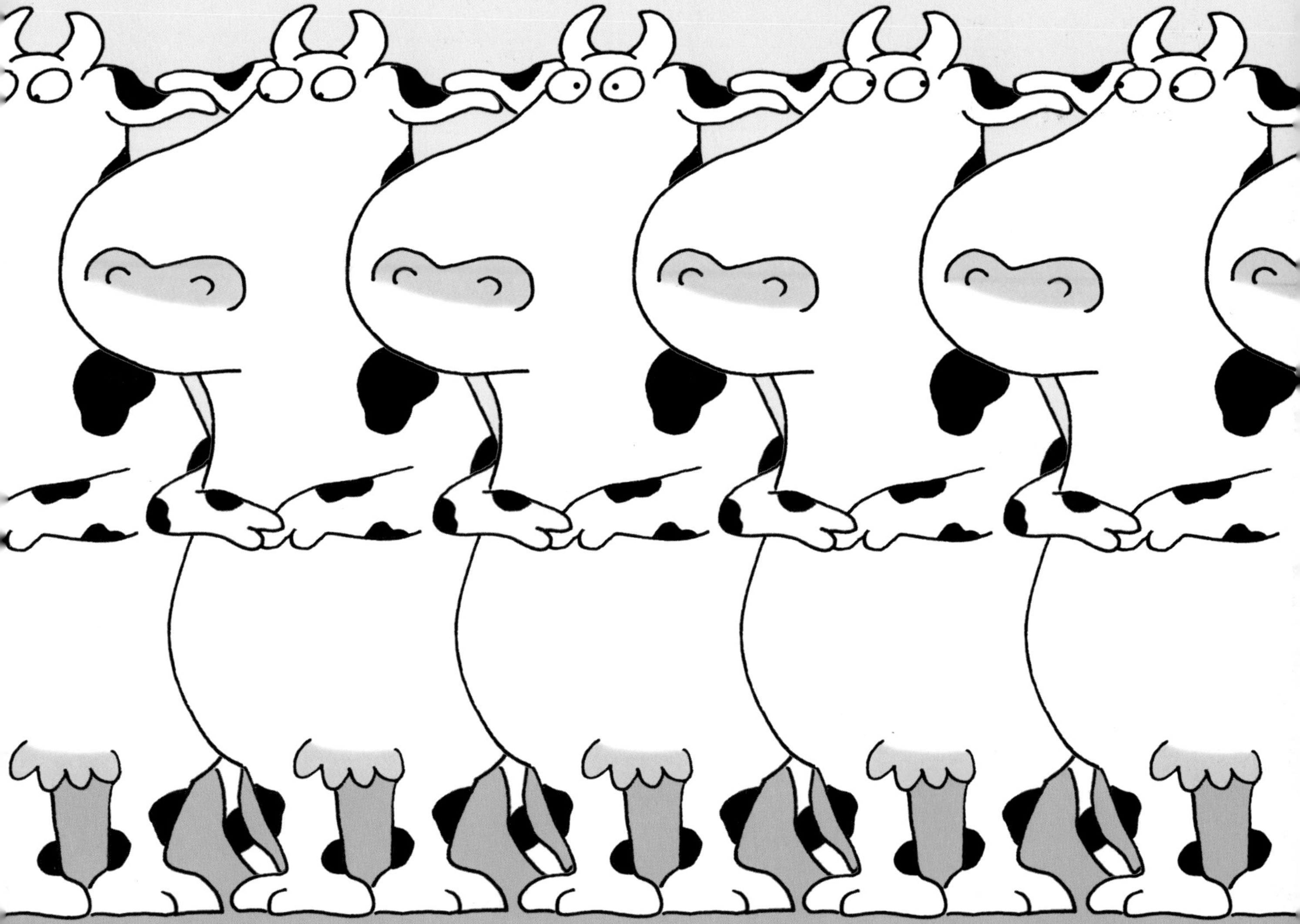

So the 137 cows and three chickens divided themselves into two groups—Team Pink and Team Green—and they lined up along each end of the dandelion field, everybody linking arms, and each team facing the other. And the game began.

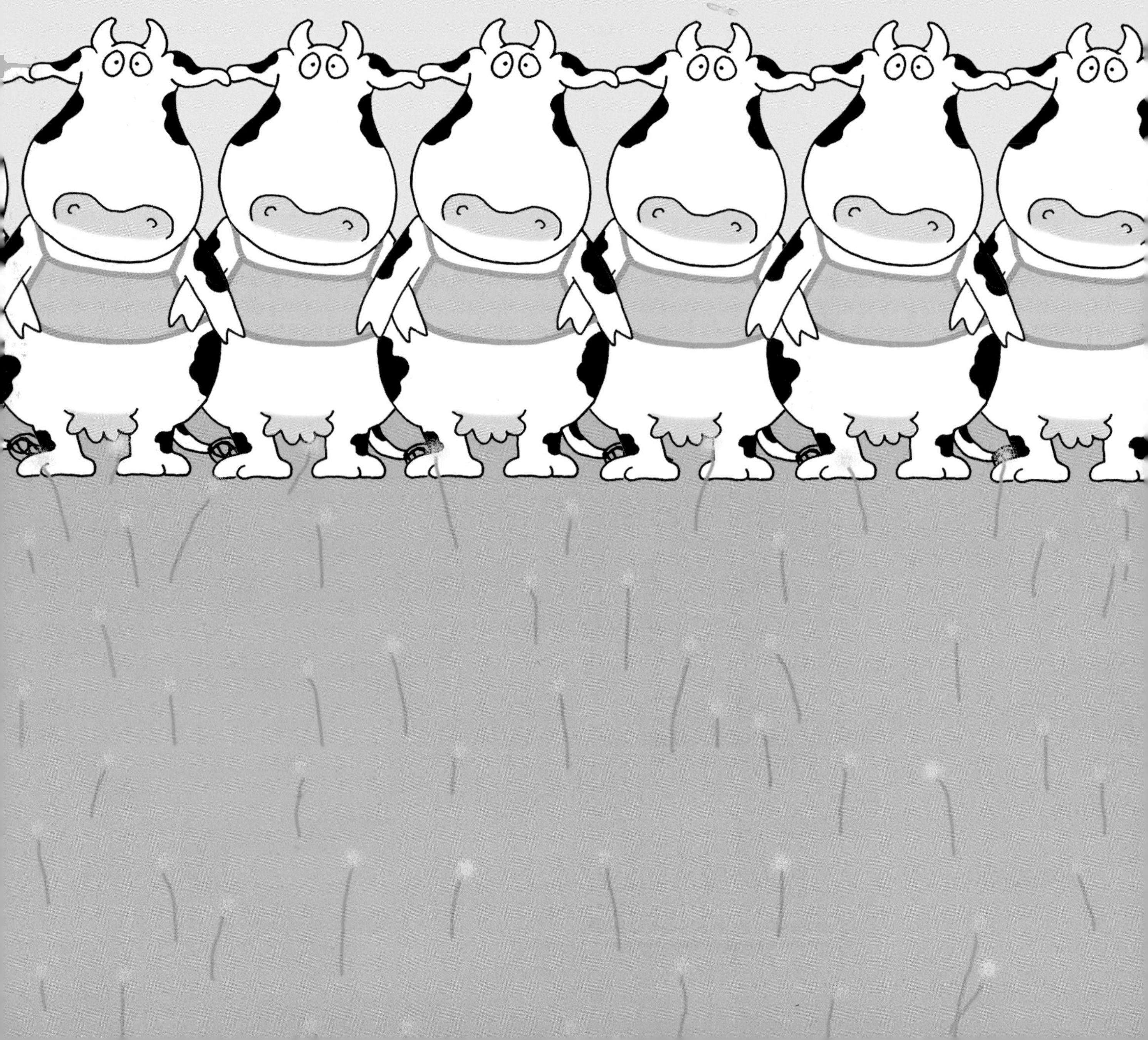

"RED ROVER, RED ROVER, LET WALTER COME OVER!"

called out Louise from the middle of the Team Pink line

and Walter took off from the Team Green side and ran as fast as he could toward Team Pink. But he could not break through their line, so he was "captured," and had to join Team Pink.

Now it was the other team's turn.

"RED ROVER, RED ROVER, LET TRIXIE COME OVER!"

called out Ezra from the middle of the Team Green line

and Trixie took off from the Team Pink side and ran as fast as she could toward Team Green.

She successfully broke through the line, right between Chaos and Lillian. So she took Lillian back with her to now become part of the Team Pink line.

It was Team Pink's turn again.

"RED ROVER, RED ROVER, LET TINO COME OVER!"

called out Nedly from the middle of the Team Pink line, because he didn't know any better...

I told you it wasn't a good idea.

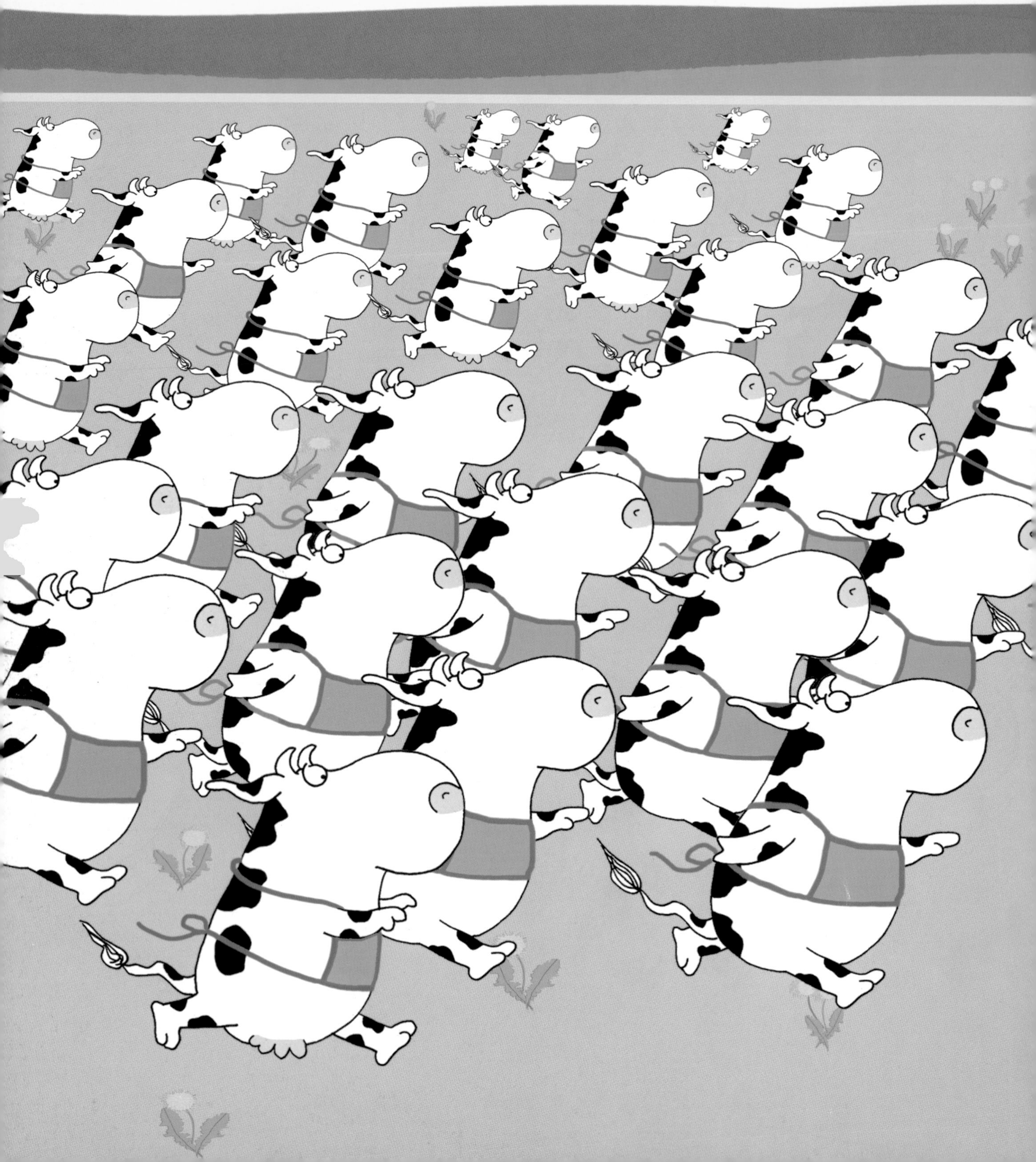

THE END

NOTES ON 

Cows are pretty much perfect just the way they are. But every once in a while, a cow may want to stand out from the herd a little. Here are the best looks for cows this season.

The **TWO-TONED TUTU** is perfect for errands about town.

24-CARAT LOGO NECKLACE by Hervé Moo

Cattle branding reinterpreted.

VINTAGE SUNGLASSES & STRIPED SILK BOWTIE

Very Hollywood.

Traditionally, gentleman cows have favored **BRASS NOSE RINGS.** It's still a strong choice.

HAND-KNIT WOOL GYM SETS are equally correct on the playground or at the opera.

COW FASHION

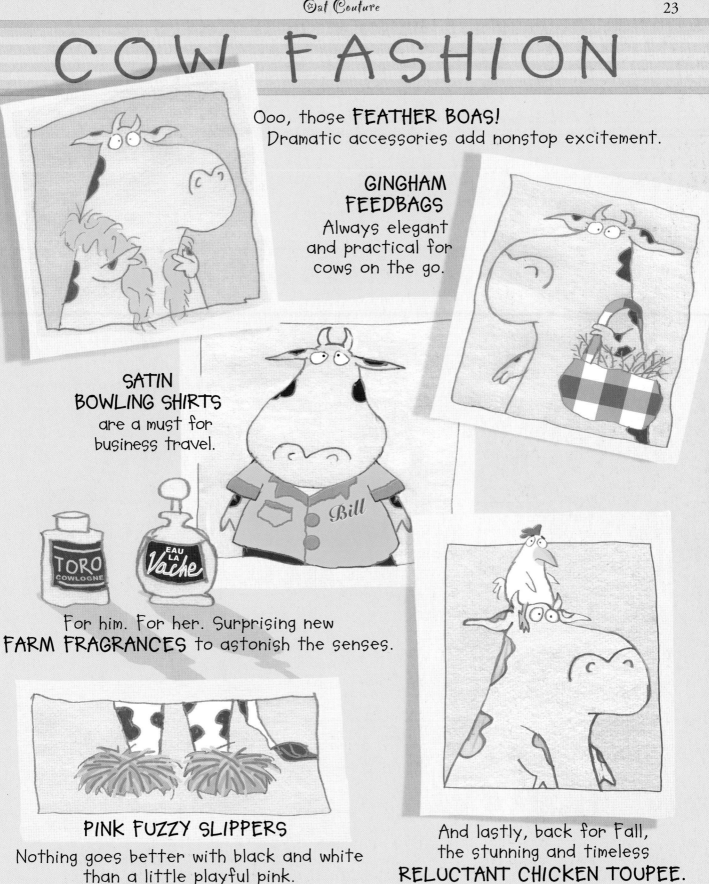

Ooo, those **FEATHER BOAS!**
Dramatic accessories add nonstop excitement.

GINGHAM FEEDBAGS
Always elegant and practical for cows on the go.

SATIN BOWLING SHIRTS
are a must for business travel.

For him. For her. Surprising new **FARM FRAGRANCES** to astonish the senses.

PINK FUZZY SLIPPERS
Nothing goes better with black and white than a little playful pink.

And lastly, back for Fall, the stunning and timeless **RELUCTANT CHICKEN TOUPEE.**

FIVE KNOCK-KNOCK JOKES!

KNOCK-KNOCK JOKE #1

KNOCK KNOCK!
Who's there?
Hawaii.
Hawaii who?
I'm fine, thank you.

[Yes, you're right. It is indeed two moo-moos in new muu-muus.]

KNOCK-KNOCK JOKE #2

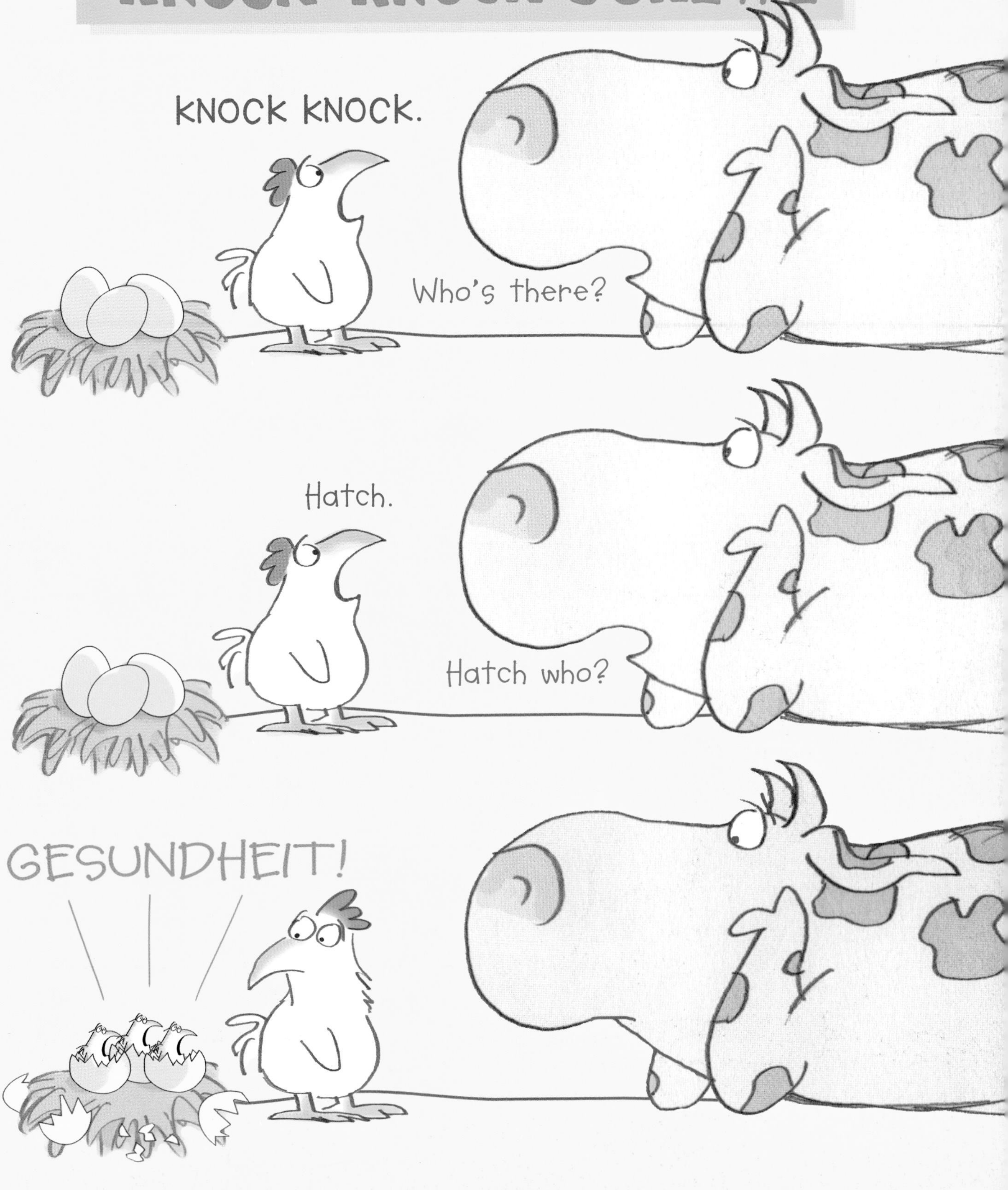

KNOCK-KNOCK JOKE #3

KNOCK-KNOCK JOKE #4

THE LAST KNOCK-KNOCK JOKE

COW LIMERICK

There's a cow
who rides waves
quite gigantic

Off the shores
of the mighty
Atlantic.

On each towering wave
He is braver than brave.

But the sight
of a mouse
makes him frantic.

FIND THE HIDDEN COWS
AMAZING COWS

We have absolutely no idea how many cows are hidden in Myra and Zeke DePig's living room. Can you find them all?

WOW!

HERE IT IS! A CLASSIC
AMAZING COW COMIC BOOK ADVENTURE
FROM THE GOLDEN AGE OF
OVERAMBITIOUS FARM ANIMALS!

No.54
APRIL 1953
10 CENTS
IC
IRRATIONAL COMICS
AMAZING
COW
Trouble on Zebblor 7

An Official AMAZING COW Adventure
TROUBLE on ZEBBLOR 7
THE FAMOUS ACME OBSERVATORY— FIVE MILES BEYOND THE SMALL TOWN OF SKIRMISH, VERMONT.
ALL OF EARTH'S TOP SCIENTISTS HAVE COME HERE ON THIS WARM SUMMER NIGHT TO DISCUSS A *SERIOUS MATTER.*
I WANT TO THANK YOU ALL FOR BEING HERE THIS EVENING.

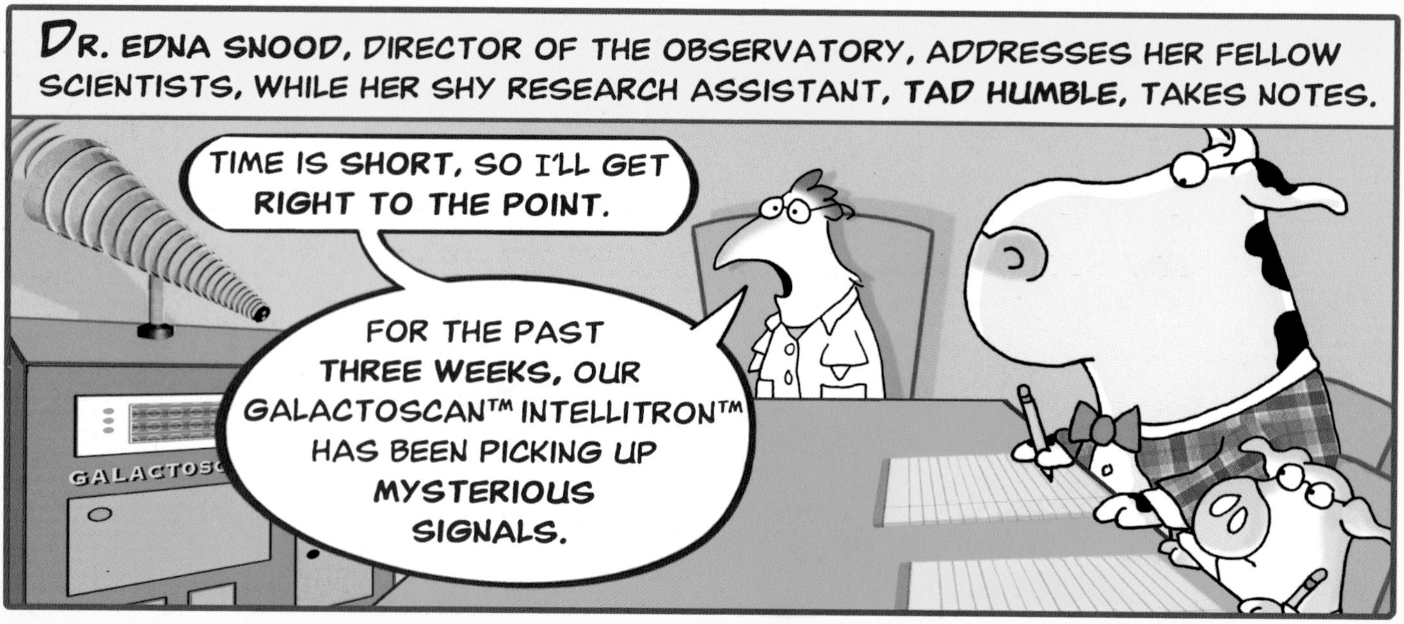
DR. EDNA SNOOD, DIRECTOR OF THE OBSERVATORY, ADDRESSES HER FELLOW SCIENTISTS, WHILE HER SHY RESEARCH ASSISTANT, TAD HUMBLE, TAKES NOTES.
TIME IS SHORT, SO I'LL GET RIGHT TO THE POINT.
FOR THE PAST THREE WEEKS, OUR GALACTOSCAN™ INTELLITRON™ HAS BEEN PICKING UP MYSTERIOUS SIGNALS.

WE BELIEVE IT MUST BE SOME SORT OF **WARNING.**
BY THE **WAVE PATTERN** OF THE SOUNDS, WE CAN TELL THAT THE MESSAGE IS **AGGRESSIVE.** BUT BEYOND THAT, I'M AFRAID WE HAVE NOT BEEN ABLE TO FIGURE OUT EXACTLY WHAT IT ALL **MEANS.**
YOU ARE THE MOST ***BRILLIANT THINKERS ON EARTH.*** THAT IS WHY WE ASKED YOU TO COME. WE NEED YOUR HELP.
MAY WE SEE THE **FIRST SLIDE,** PLEASE, TAD?
RIGHT AWAY, DR. SNOOD.
THE SHY RESEARCH ASSISTANT FLICKS ON THE SLIDE PROJECTOR AND TURNS OFF THE LIGHTS. A **PUZZLING IMAGE** COMES UP ON THE SCREEN.

BOK BOK BOK BOK BOK HONK SHOOO HONK SHOOO HONK SH...
KWAK KWAK KWAK KWAK KWAK
BOK BOK BOK BOK BOK HONK SHOOO HONK SHOOO HONK SH...
KWAK KWAK KWAK KWAK KWAK
BOK BOK BOK BOK BOK HONK SHOOO HONK SHOOO HONK SH...
KWAK KWAK KWAK KWAK KWAK
BOK BOK BOK BOK BOK HONK SHOOO HONK
HONK SH...
KWAK KWAK KWAK KWAK
ZEBBLOR SECTOR TRANSMISSION 16:04:33:12
HERE WE HAVE A PRINTOUT OF THE STRANGE NOISE PATTERN.
IF YOU STUDY THIS PATTERN CAREFULLY, YOU'LL NOTICE...
SUDDENLY—
BLAM!
A VERY LOUD NOISE FILLS THE AIR, SENDING A SURGE OF FEAR THROUGH THE ROOM.
YIKES!
TURN ON THE LIGHTS!
WHAT WAS THAT?
KNOCK KNOCK.
WHO'S THERE?
TAD QUICKLY TURNS THE LIGHTS BACK ON. DR. MERGAN GANSER, A QUIET AUDIOLOGIST FROM ZURICH, HOLDS A STRANGE OBJECT.
OH. SORRY.

I JUST SUDDENLY FELT LIKE YELLING 'BLAM' INTO THIS ABSURDLY POWERFUL MEGAPHONE. PLEASE CONTINUE.
THE SCIENTISTS ACCEPT DR. GANSER'S APOLOGY, AND THEY ALL DECIDE TO BREAK FOR A QUICK GAME OF HIDE-AND-GO-SEEK IN THE TELESCOPE ROOM...
EVERYONE, THAT IS, EXCEPT SHY RESEARCH ASSISTANT TAD HUMBLE, WHO PONDERS HIS CAREFUL NOTES.
HMM... I WONDER.
AREN'T YOU COMING, TAD?
DR. SNOOD, MAY I HAVE YOUR PERMISSION TO GO OUT AND DO SOME QUICK RESEARCH INSTEAD?
OH. YES. OF COURSE.
TAD DASHES OFF TO A NEARBY CLOSET. ELEVEN SECONDS LATER, HE EMERGES AS...
NEARBY CLOSET

...AMAZING COW!
NEARBY CLOSET
COW OF TOMORROW. FRIEND OF THE DOWNTRODDEN. FASHION ICON.
AMAZING COW SLIPS QUIETLY TO AN OPEN WINDOW, AND LEAPS OUT BOLDLY INTO THE WARM NIGHT AIR.
HE FLIES SWIFTLY THROUGH THE DARK SKY...
...AWAY FROM EARTH, BEYOND THE PULL OF GRAVITY...
...ON INTO OUTER SPACE.

WHERE IN THE UNIVERSE IS AMAZING COW GOING?
AH! TO ZEBBLOR 8, SOMETIMES KNOWN AS "PLANET OF THE ANNOYING DUCKS."
OH! IT'S AMAZING COW!
YES, IT IS I!
I NOTICE THAT YOU ARE ALL IN PAJAMAS EVEN THOUGH IT IS THE MIDDLE OF THE DAY HERE ON ZEBBLOR 8.
UM. YES.
MAY I ASSUME THAT THE CHICKENS OF ZEBBLOR 7 ARE ALSO ALL IN PAJAMAS?

NO ONE ANSWERS.
I CAN FLY OVER THERE TO FIND OUT FOR MYSELF.
OKAY, YES! THE CHICKENS ARE ALL IN PAJAMAS, TOO!
AND MAY I ASSUME THAT YOU HAVE STARTED A *SNORE WAR?*
NO ONE ANSWERS.

I CAN FLY OVER...
OKAY, YES! WE HAVE STARTED A SNORE WAR!
AND MAY I ASSUME THAT THE FAMOUS AUDIOLOGIST DR. MERGAN GANSER...
YES! DR. GANSER PAYS US TO KEEP THE CHICKENS AWAKE SO THAT THEY WILL HAVE TO BUY THE *EARPLUGS* HE INVENTED!
JUST AS I SUSPECTED. PLEASE DON'T DO IT ANY MORE.
OKAY!
CHICKENS HAVE EARS?
AND NOW I'M OFF TO SEE THE CHICKENS. FAREWELL.
THE DUCKS STAND SPELL-BOUND AS AMAZING COW ZOOMS AWAY...

OUR HERO NOW LANDS ON ZEBBLOR 7, PLANET OF THE REALLY TIRED CHICKENS.
HOORAY FOR AMAZING COW!
I SEE YOU ALL HAVE YOUR ANTENNAE UP. WERE YOU EAVESDROPPING ON MY MEETING WITH THE DUCKS?
YES! YES, WE WERE!
CHICKENS OF ZEBBLOR, IT IS NOT POLITE TO...
ZZZZZZZZZZZZZZZZZZZZZZZZ...
...BUT THE CHICKENS AREN'T LISTENING. THEY HAVE ALL FALLEN ASLEEP.

AMAZING COW NOW LEAVES ZEBBLOR 7 AND RETURNS SPEEDILY TO THE ACME OBSERVATORY, WHERE THE SCIENTISTS' HIDE-AND-SEEK GAME IS JUST WRAPPING UP.
OLLIE OLLIE OXEN FREEEEEE!
IN ONE TERRIFIC SWOOP, AMAZING COW ENTERS THROUGH THE ROOF HATCH AND ALIGHTS IN FRONT OF THE SCIENTISTS.
AMAZING COW!
GOOD EVENING. WHERE IS DR. GANSER, PLEASE?
WE DON'T KNOW.
HE MUST HAVE FOUND A REALLY GOOD HIDING PLACE.
HMM... IT IS A GOOD HIDING PLACE...
[AMAZING C-THRU VISION!]
... BUT NOT GOOD ENOUGH!
ULP!

PARDON ME FOR RUSHING OFF THIS WAY, BUT I MUST TAKE DR. GANSER TO AN APPOINTMENT WITH THE OUTER SPACE POLICE. GOOD-BYE FOR NOW.
THE SCIENTISTS WATCH IN WONDER AS AMAZING COW FLIES OFF INTO THE NIGHT, PULLING ALONG DR. GANSER BY MEANS OF THE AMAZING TRACTOR BEAM.
LATER—
...AND IT TURNS OUT THAT DR. GANSER WAS BEHIND THE WHOLE THING! SOMEHOW OR OTHER, AMAZING COW FIGURED IT ALL OUT. AND THEN HE FLEW TO THE ZEBBLOR SECTOR TO PUT A STOP TO THE SNORE WAR!
GOSH!
IT'S A SHAME YOU COULDN'T GET BACK HERE IN TIME TO MEET AMAZING COW, TAD.
YES, DR. SNOOD, I'M SORRY I MISSED HIM. IT WOULD HAVE BEEN PRETTY SWELL TO SHAKE HIS HOOF. THOUGH SOMETIMES I FEEL AS IF I ALREADY KNOW HIM.
THE END

DVERTISEMENT • ADVERTISEMENT • ADVERTISEMENT • ADVERTISEMENT • ADVERTISEMENT • ADVERTISEMENT • OKAY, NOT REALLY

If you buy *just one book* on decorating with livestock, this should possibly be that book.

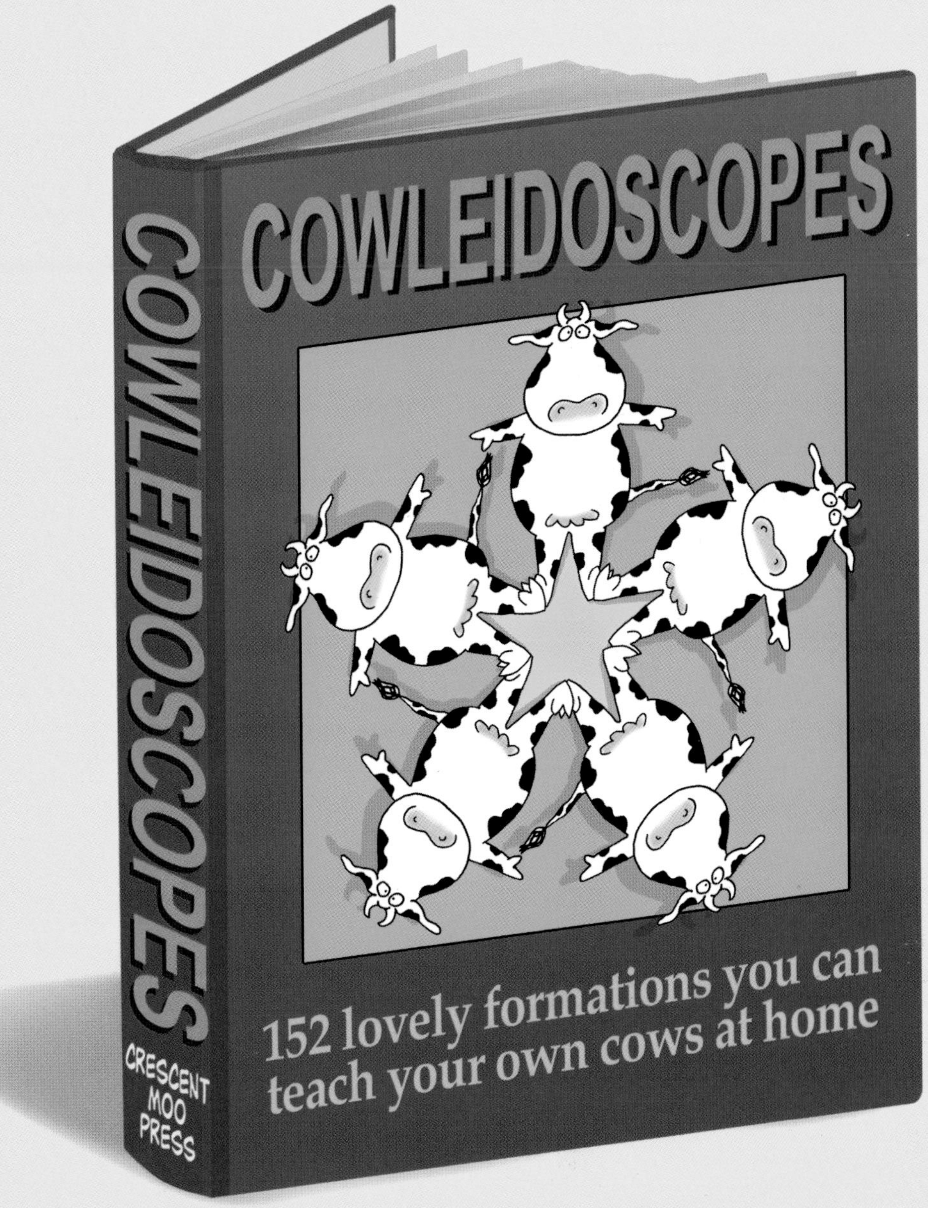

AVAILABLE WHEREVER BOOKS LIKE THIS ARE SOLD

The Definitive Performance

of the Timeless Song

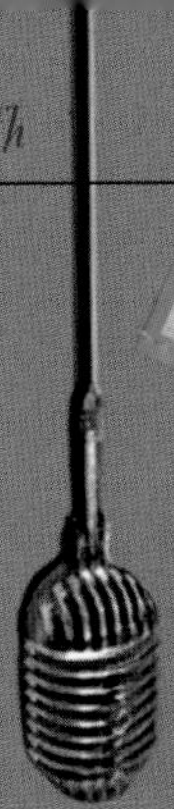

It Had to Be Moo

It had to be Moo.
It had to be Moo.
No other sound is half as profound,
And somehow I knew.
That magical MMM that drifts into OOO.
So wonderfully low, so tried and so true.
It had to be Moo.

It had to be Moo.
Just had to be Moo.
Not oink or meow.
Forget bow wow wow.
Cock-a-doodle won't do.

They can keep every quack,
Every baa, every neigh.
You can take them all back.
There's just
one word I'll say—
It had to be Moo.
Marvelous Moo.
It had to be...
MOOOOO.

COW RIDDLE

Her face was bright.
Now, the slightest smile.
And soon she must
Go away for a while.

Sometimes I begin
To call out her name.
She is ever-changing.
And ever the same.

Who is she?

FOR THE ANSWER,
PLEASE TURN THE PAGE

DAY 1
"Her face was bright."
DAY 12
"Now, the slightest smile."
DAY 15
"And soon she must
Go away for a while."
DAY 20
MOOOO...
"Sometimes I begin
To call out her name."
DAY 24
"She is ever-changing."
DAY 30
"And ever the same."
Who is she?

ANSWER:

The moon.

Nope! SORRY! WRONG answer!
The CORRECT answer is
Zelda Q. Ningleberry
of Frumbleston-upon-Snub.

Day One at Cow Camp

Counselor Phil:

DO you WANT to BE A COW?

DO you WANT to DO IT NOW?

BE A COW!

DO IT NOW!

Everybody go MOOOOOOOOOOOO!

A little bit louder: MOOOOOOOO!

Moo-bitty MOO!

Quackitty quack!

Oops.

Sorry.

Please stop.

No, really.

Campers:

→ YES, we WANT to BE A COW!

→ YES, we WANT to DO IT NOW!

→ BE A COW!

→ DO IT NOW!

→ MOOOOOOOOOOOOO!

→ MOOOOOOOOO!

→ Moo-bitty MOO!

→ Quackitty quack!

→ Oops!

→ Sorry!

→ Please stop!

→ No, really!

FAMOUS BARNYARD COMPOSERS

Wolfgang Amadeus
MOOZART

Piotr Ilyich
TCHAIKOWSKY

Ludwig van
BEETHOOVEN

Johann Sebastian
BOCKBOCKBOCK

COW MYTH

"The Contest"

COW MYTH

In ancient times there lived a hopeful young cow. Her real name was Mnemomenomenomene* but everyone called her "Izzy" for reasons that are now unclear. Though honestly, YOU try calling: "Yoo hoo, Mnemomenomenomene!" And don't even TALK to me about spelling it.

*nem–AH–min–AH–min–AH–min–ee

One breezy day in early autumn, enormous posters went up all over town (Athens, I'm guessing, though Fort Lauderdale is also a strong possibility) announcing a major contest.

WRITE A STADIUM CHEER
to honor
ZOOSE
AWESOME GOD OF THE SKY
Winner gets a nifty laurel wreath
ZOOSE
Contest is open to all citizens of Athens or maybe Fort Lauderdale

Izzy was captivated. She loved to write, and had long dreamed of taking part in such an event.

She signed up right away.

Over the next three weeks, Izzy spent many, many hours trying out various ideas for a great Stadium Cheer.

She hardly ate.
She hardly slept.
She rarely went outside.

But nothing she came up with seemed very Izzy at all.

By the evening before the big contest, Izzy had gotten nowhere. She was discouraged, and concerned. She simply couldn't imagine what she would do tomorrow when her turn to recite came around.

"Well," thought Izzy, "maybe now it's time to stop striving." So she put down her pencil, and made herself a nice hot cup of clover tea.

Then she went outside to the orchard. And as the moon was rising, Izzy stood among the ripening apples and played "Stardust" on her aulos.

She held the lovely last note just a little longer than usual. Then she listened. The sound echoed from the hills all around, and faded away into the chill September night.

Izzy went back inside and carefully placed her aulos onto its cushion. She was peacefully happy. "One simple sustain, and suddenly everything is right," she thought.

As she got herself ready for bed, she suddenly stopped and said out loud, "Oh, wait! I know what to do!"

She quickly went to her desk, took pencil in hoof, and wrote with gusto and purpose.

Before she went to sleep, Izzy took a moment to read through her work one last time. She was pleased. She knew she was ready for tomorrow's contest. She had written an excellent Stadium Cheer—one that was strong yet understated, elegant yet simple. Very Izzy.

Then she slept.

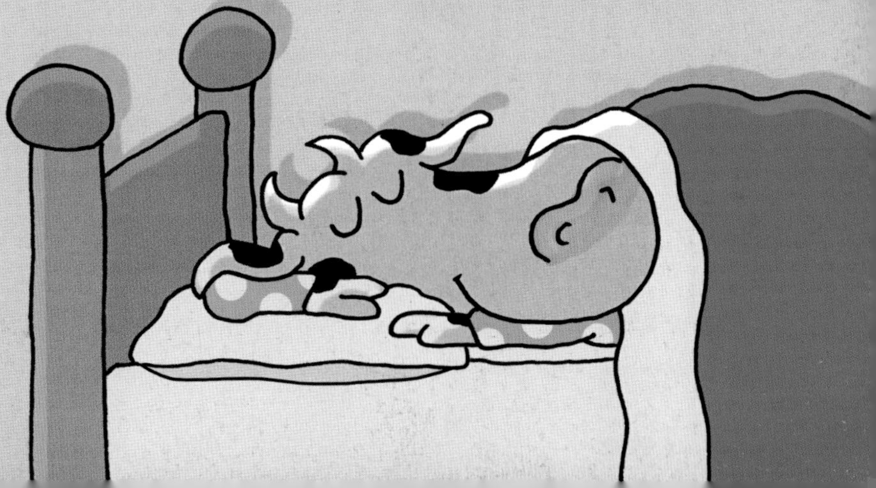

The next day, the competition began promptly at XII o'clock. The stadium was completely sold out.

The first contestant, a popular chicken, walked briskly to the center of the field. The crowd hushed, and in a loud, clear voice, the chicken recited her Stadium Cheer:

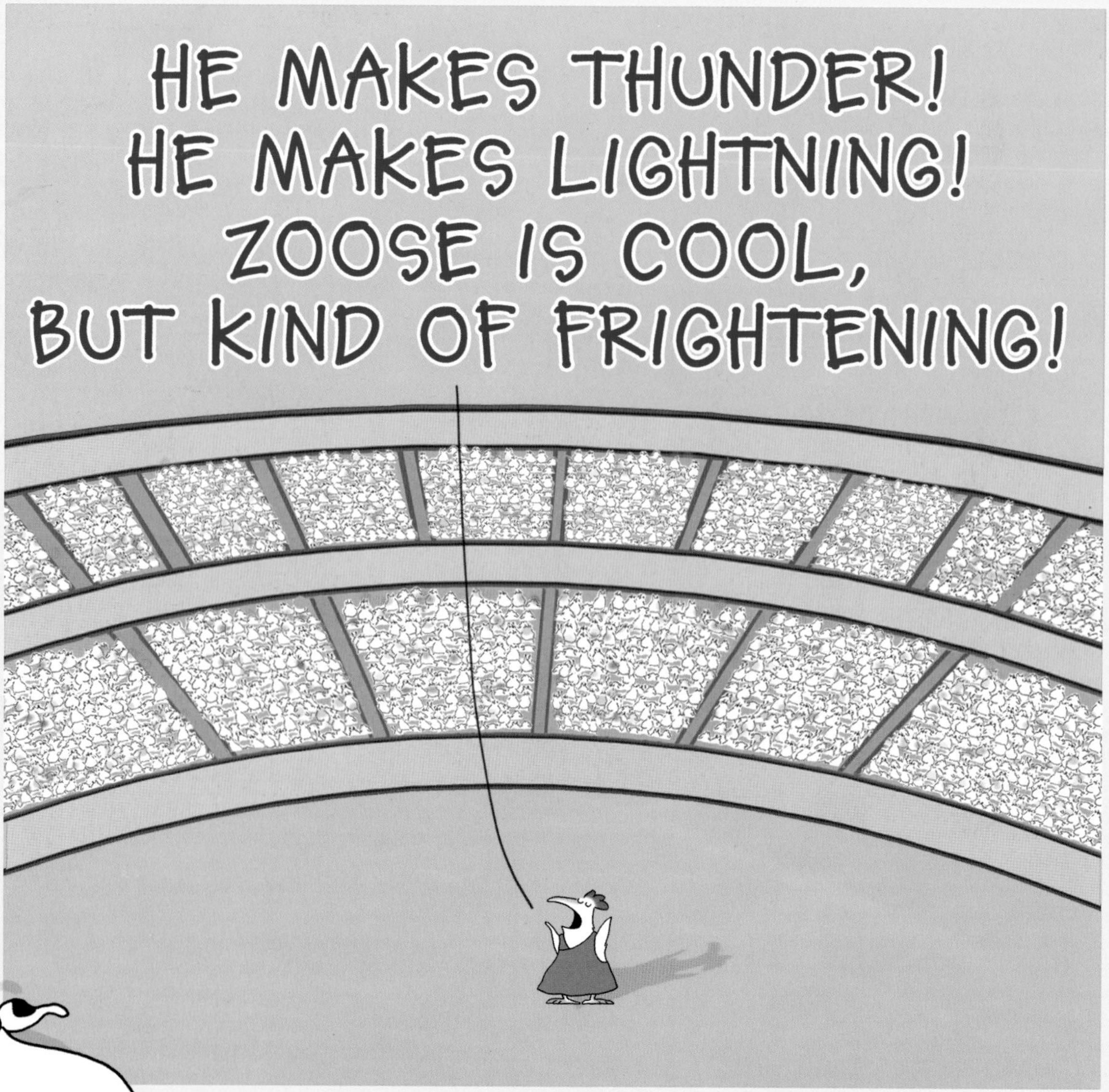

HE MAKES THUNDER!
HE MAKES LIGHTNING!
ZOOSE IS COOL,
BUT KIND OF FRIGHTENING!

The crowd applauded enthusiastically.

"That cheer was good," thought Izzy. "But I think perhaps my cheer is a little spiffier."

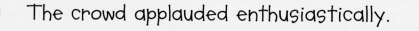

Now it was time for the next contestant. A heroic pig stepped confidently into place. The stadium grew silent again. The pig spoke out boldly:

WHO'S THE BEST IMMORTAL MOOSE?
ZIPPITY ZANG!
IT MUST BE ZOOSE!

Loud was the applause for this impressive performance.

"That was a very fine cheer as well," thought Izzy. "But now it's my turn to show what I can do."

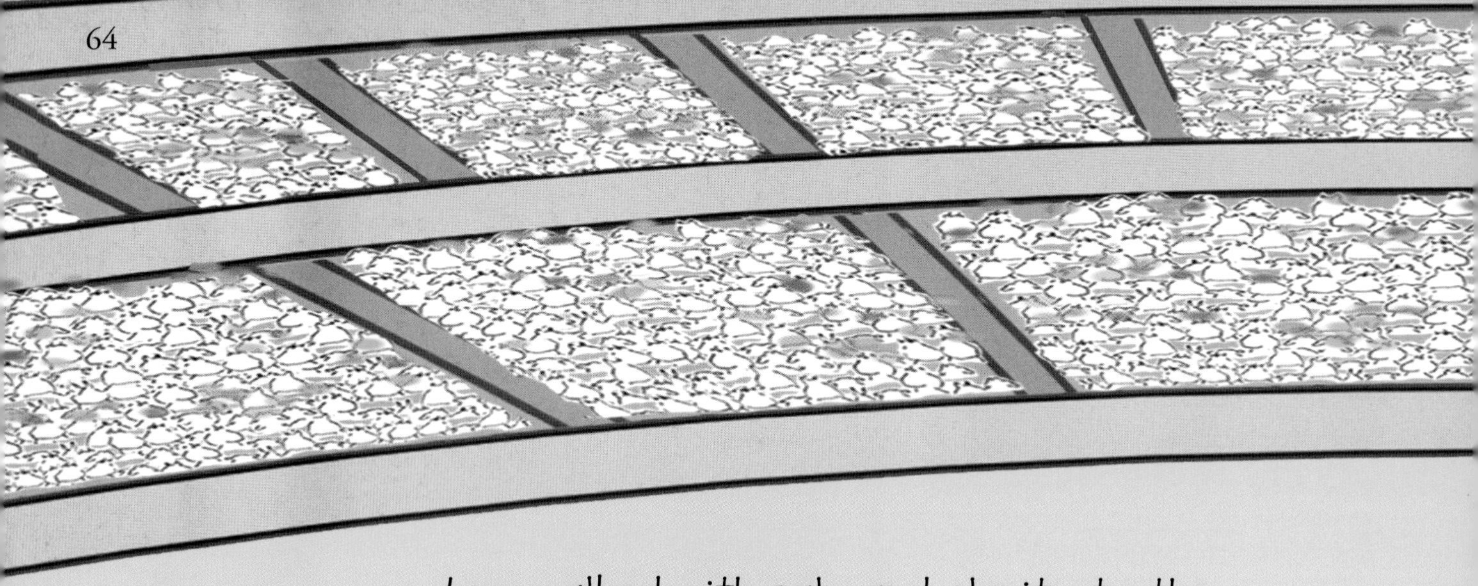

Izzy walked with calm and clarity to the center of the enormous arena. She closed her eyes, and felt the sweet afternoon breeze gently loft her ears.

She waited a moment.

Then in a low, strong, resonant voice, she intoned—as one deep and pure sustained note—the simple and elegant Stadium Cheer which she had taken so much care to create.

ZOOOOOOOSE.

One word. Izzy's cheer was just one word.

The entire crowd sat awestruck as the stadium reverberated with the glorious sound.

Then, spontaneously, forty-seven thousand joyful voices answered the cheer right back.

ZOOOOOOSE!

The day went dark and a streak of lightning illuminated the entire sky. Everyone in the entire stadium (except for one duck) knew what this meant—

ZOOSE HIMSELF HAD DECLARED IZZY THE WINNER!

And so Izzy was presented with the laurel wreath.

It was delicious.

THE END

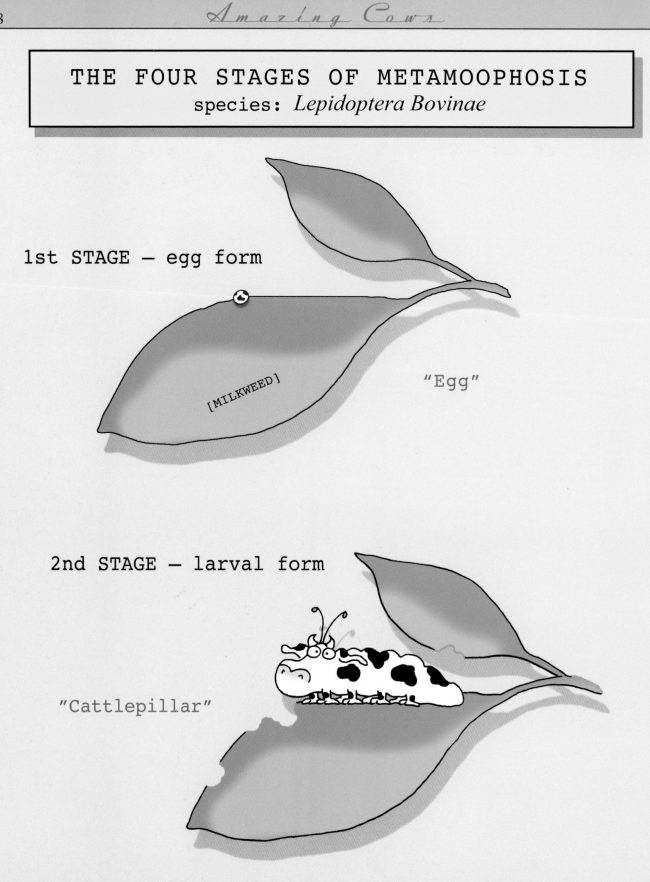

THE FOUR STAGES OF METAMOOPHOSIS
species: *Lepidoptera Bovinae*

1st STAGE – egg form

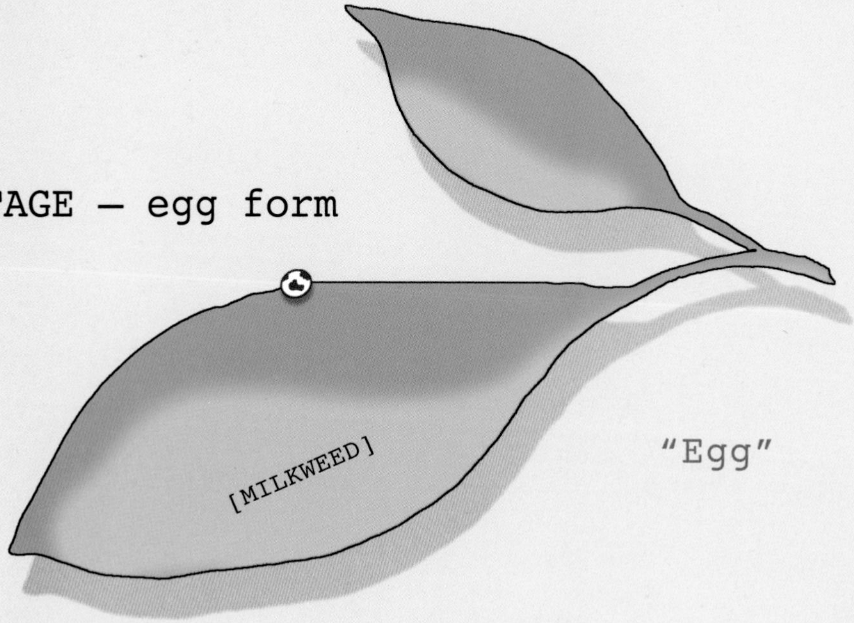

"Egg"

2nd STAGE – larval form

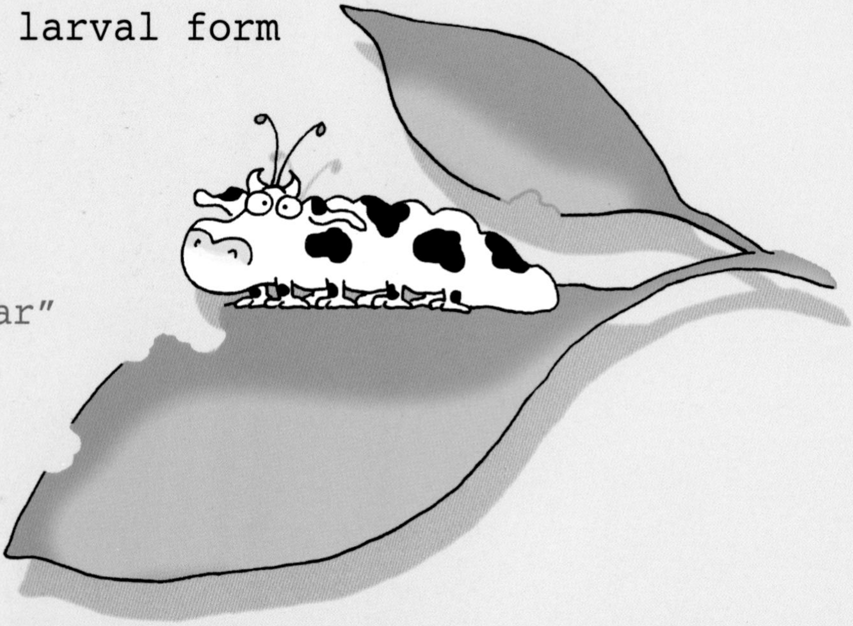

"Cattlepillar"

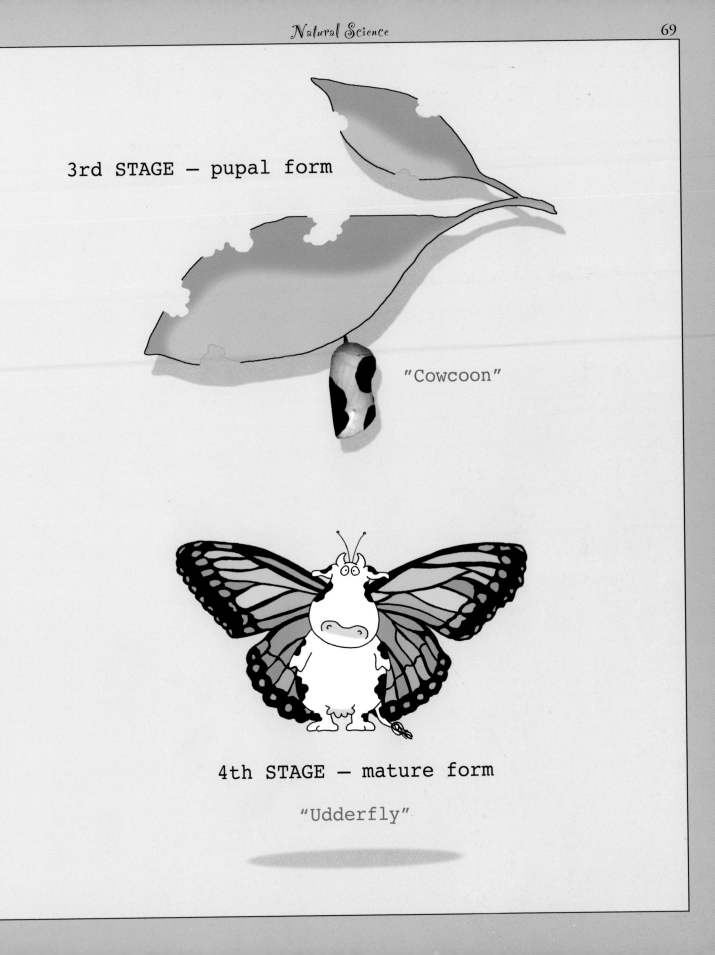

3rd STAGE – pupal form

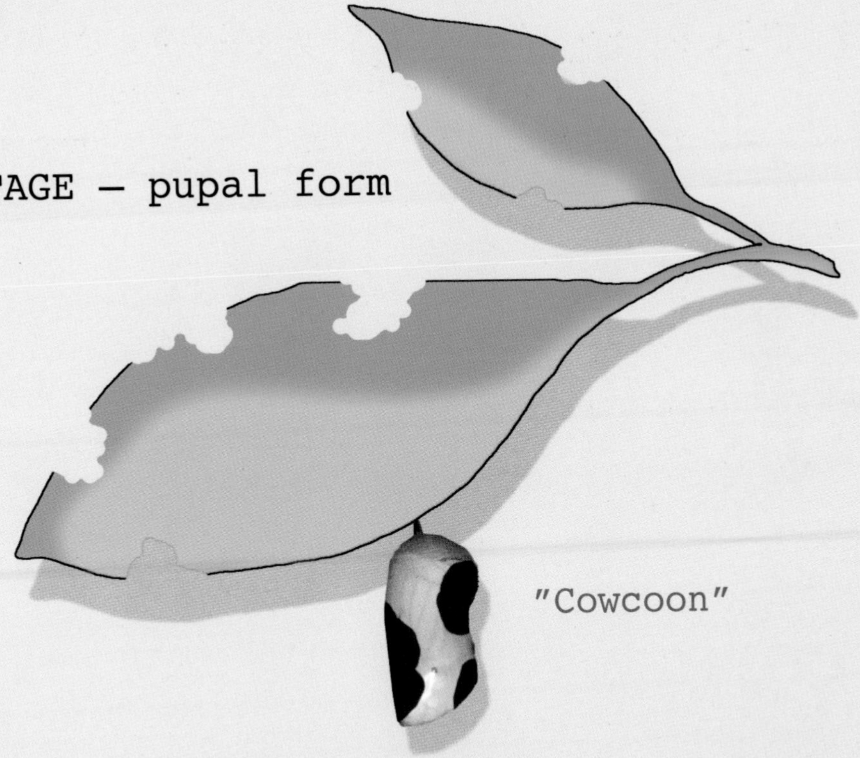

"Cowcoon"

4th STAGE – mature form

"Udderfly"

BARYSHNICOWS

Once they stood contented
Through simple summer days
In meadowlands of green familiar clover.
But someone from the city
Taught them tour-jetés.
And now it seems those simple days are over.

3 MORE COW JOKES!

Q: What is a stampede of cows called?

A: Um, it's called a stampede.

Q: Oh FINE. What's another name for a stampede of cows?

A: Udder chaos.

Q: What do you call a perfect cow civilization?

A: Mootopia.

Greetings from
COW PLANET
"Home of the Amazing Singing Cows"
© Boynton

Q: What do you call a cow who loves bluegrass music, avoids camping trips, and wears green glasses?

A: Bob.

Hard Rock Cows: Docile by day. Edgy by night.

COW AND PIG STORY

"The Perfect Day"

COW and PIG STORY

There once lived a cow and a pig who were very good friends. They most enjoyed slow walks together when they would talk about many things—music, art, the weather, a really loud chicken they both knew, and so on.

One day while they were strolling along, the pig said to the cow, "Violet, I always cherish our walks. But next time, I would like you to come and try my favorite thing in the whole wide world."

"What a nice idea, Morton," said Violet. "What is your favorite thing?"

"Lying around all day long in the mud!" replied the pig.

"Oh," said the cow. "Oh."

They made a plan to meet at the mud puddle the very next day.

So the next morning, Violet ate a breakfast of 35 pancakes topped with grass, and she arrived at the mud puddle promptly at eight.

"Welcome!" said Morton happily, and he strode directly into the puddle, rolled over in the mud three times, and lay down snout–upward, a blissful smile on his face.

"How is it?" asked Violet, trying hard to sound perky.

"Wonderful!" answered the muddy pig. "Come on in!"

Violet tiptoed into the puddle, and she slowly lay down, muzzle-upward.

"Ahhh," she said. "Wet dirt."

"YES!" agreed Morton.

"And what happens now?" asked Violet in a merry manner.

"We stay just like this till sundown!" replied the pig.

"Swell," said Violet.

And that's what they did.

At sunset, the two friends stood up.

"Thank you for inviting me, Morton," said Violet.

"Thank you for coming, Violet," said Morton.

They shook hooves, said goodbye, and went home.

Violet took a long hot bath.

On their customary walk the next day, Morton and Violet talked about travel, cooking, the theater, a very confusing duck they both knew, and so on.

And then the cow said to the pig, "Morton, I always cherish our walks together. But next time, I would like you to come and try my favorite thing in the whole wide world."

"What a nice idea, Violet," said the pig.
"What is your favorite thing?"

"Standing around all day in the field, chewing grass," replied the cow.

"Gosh," said Morton. "Gosh."
And he smiled what he hoped looked like a delighted smile.

And so two friends agreed to meet at the meadow the very next morning.

The next morning, Morton ate a fabulous breakfast of 27 pancakes topped with garbage.

He arrived at the meadow promptly at seven o'clock.

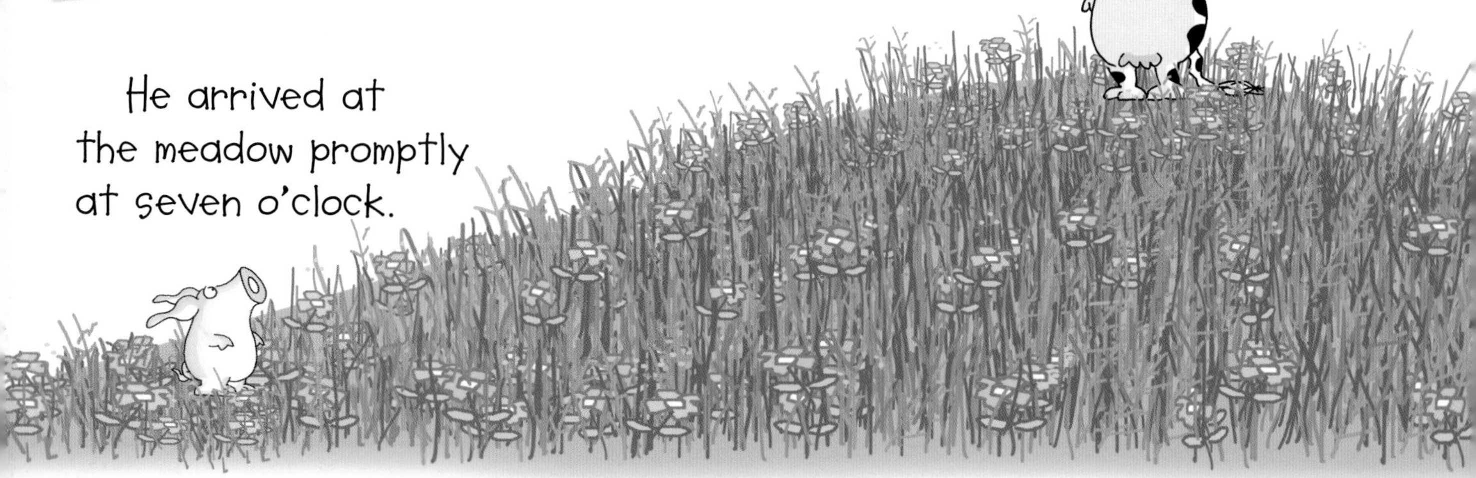

"Welcome!" called out Violet from the hilltop. She picked a large bunch of grass, and put all of it into her mouth. Then she waved happily at Morton, and motioned him to come join her.

Morton scurried to Violet's side, and picked two hoofuls of grass. He couldn't bring himself to actually put it in his mouth, but Violet didn't notice.

And there they stood for hours and hours, gazing into the distance. Now and then Violet would murmur a happy "Mooooo."

As would Morton.

Just before sunset, who should happen to come along but Baxter the really loud chicken and Wendell the confusing duck.

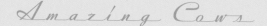

"HEY THERE!" yelled Baxter. "WHAT ARE YOU GUYS DOING?"

"Speak to me of dishwashing liquid," said Wendell softly.

"WE ARE WATCHING THE SUN GO DOWN," the cow called back.

"MAKE ROOM FOR US!"

shouted Baxter.

"Blatt!" said Wendell.

And the four animals stood side by side, facing west as the sun slowly set.

Which would have been fine, except that the whole time the chicken was yelling

"GOING!...GOING!...GOING!...GOING!..."

and Wendell was singing a slow, sad song about static electricity.

When at last the sun had set, Baxter shouted "GONE!" and Wendell shouted "LOCATE THE SAFETY VALVE!" Then the loud chicken and the confusing duck ran off as fast as you can imagine.

Now the evening was lovely and still.

"You know, Violet," said Morton quietly, "my favorite thing about this day was seeing you where you love to be."

"And my favorite thing about our puddle day," replied Violet, "was seeing you where you love to be."

The cow and the pig stood for a moment in silence, enjoying the afterglow of the sunset and the gentle joy of true friendship.

"And my second-favorite part of today," said the pig, "was when the chicken and the duck went away."

"Mine, too," said Violet. "Mine, too."

THE END

ANOTHER COW LIMERICK

I know a fine cow
named Pierre
Who says he can sleep
anywhere.
He managed to
snooze
While 300 kazoos
Played "Boléro."
I envy Pierre.

NOTE

You can listen to "Boléro Completely Unraveled" by following the download directions inside the back cover. But we don't recommend it.

THE END! THE COW BOOK IS OVER!

"You used to cling to me,
Give a zing to me.
Tell me, my laundry,
What went wrong?
Oh, the
static electricity's
gone..."